Quick Adjustments

Micro-Stories

Robert Scotellaro

BLUE LIGHT PRESS ◆ 1ST WORLD PUBLISHING

1ST WORLD
PUBLISHING

SAN FRANCISCO ◆ FAIRFIELD ◆ DELHI

Quick Adjustments

1ST WORLD LIBRARY
106 South Court Street
Fairfield, Iowa 52556
www.1stworldpublishing.com

BLUE LIGHT PRESS
www.bluelightpress.com
Email: bluelightpress@aol.com

BOOK & COVER DESIGN
Melanie Gendron
melaniegendron999@gmail.com

COVER ART
Up in the Air
from iStock with permission (2023)

AUTHOR PHOTO
Diana Scott

FIRST EDITION

Library of Congress Cataloging-in-Publication Data

ISBN: 978-1-4218-3553-2

ALSO BY ROBERT SCOTELLARO

Fiction

God in a Can
Ways to Read the World
What Are the Chances?
Nothing Is Ever One Thing
Bad Motel
What We Know So Far
Measuring the Distance

Poetry

After the Revolution
The Night Sings A Capella
Rhapsody of Fallen Objects
My Father's Cadillac
Early Love Poems of Genghis Khan
Blinded by Halos
East Harlem Poems

Anthology

NEW MICRO:
Exceptionally Short Fiction
Co-edited with James Thomas

For Children

Snail Stampede
Dancing with Frankenstein
Carla and the Greedy Merchant
The Terrible Storm

"We have to continually be jumping off cliffs and developing our wings on the way down."

– Kurt Vonnegut

ACKNOWLEDGMENTS

Grateful acknowledgment is made to the following publications in which these works or earlier versions previously appeared:

"We Make Do" *South Florida Poetry Journal*
"Reading by Ghost Light" *The Journal of Compressed Creative Arts*
"The Intruder" *South Florida Poetry Journal*
"Viva Las Vegas" *South Florida Poetry Journal*
"A Rush of Shadows" *Blue Fifth Review; What Are the Chances?*
"Incredible Figure Fours" *Fictive Dream*
"Fire Walker" Flash: *The International Short-Short Story Magazine; What We Know So Far*
"Diversity Takes, What We Can Only Hope, Is a Vacation" *South Florida Poetry Journal*
"Bug Porn" *Best Small Fictions 2016 (Guest Edited by Stuart Dybek), What We Know So Far*
"Metaphors Incognito" *South Florida Poetry Journal*
"The Polygamist's Three Wives" *Mojave River Review*
"Leo the Leviathan" *Postcard Shorts; What We Know So Far*
"Superhero" *Flash: The International Short-Short Story Magazine*
"so much depends…" *The Journal of Compressed Creative Arts; What We Know So Far*
"Bomb Shelter" *10 by 10*
"Saw Blade" *The San Franciscan; Measuring the Distance*
"Gravity's Big Hands" *Pure Slush "Ambition" Anthology*
"Leaning In" *NANO Fiction; NANO Fiction Podcast; What Are the Chances?*
"Interpreter of Dreams" *6S Anthology* (edited by Lydia Davis); *What We Know So Far*
"The Lion's Cage" *Poetrybay*
"The Short Happy Life of Uncle Sal" *6S Anthology* (edited by Lydia Davis); *Measuring the Distance*
"The Flying Blunders" *Fictive Dream*
"Cold Light" *Camroc Press Review; What We Know So Far*
"Ledge at the Edge of the World" *10 by 10*
"Sonic Boom" *DOGZPLOT*
"A Home for Monsters" *South Florida Poetry Journal*
"Newfound" *Pure Slush Anthology*
"All the People We Have Ever Been" *Poetrybay*

for Diana

CONTENTS

We Make Do

I looked out the window and the moon was only a few feet away with all those craters and that broken-egg-yellow light in afterglow. The kid's swing set was crushed and all our furniture rearranged a bit from the impact, but Rita brought in a bottle of wine, two glasses, and said how romantic it was. I told her I never knew gravity had such big hands. Filling the glasses, she said she always wanted a swimming pool, pointing to one of the smaller craters. Lights were clicking on around the neighborhood and car alarms were screaming, but damn if Rita didn't look good in that sexy white nightie which was golden now. Tomorrow I could break out the garden hose and fill the crater so Rita and I could do some laps in those hot swimsuits we hardly fit in anymore. And the kids could splash around in it, and hell, even though I kind of missed the way things were, with it up in the sky and all, this was beginning to look like things were going to work out just fine.

The Whatchamacallit

He made balloon animals for the tourists at Pier 39 in San Francisco. Dachshunds and rabbits, and occasionally an amorphous and elaborate "thing" he called a whatchamacallit. (Which was open to interpretation.) His one squeaky plunge at being an artist. He dated my sister at the time and told me once he felt like the head of an unstruck match with all that fire inside. I asked him one day what his "whatchamacallit" was and he just laughed. Blew up a few long skinny balloons and with a robust twisting fury, created something extraordinary. Something, that if it had not been made of that taut, ephemeral skin, was made of something durable and lasting, might be showcased in a gallery or museum. He smiled and put the thing on the coffee table, then clicked on the TV to watch the game. But all I could watch was that complex and extraordinary construction with the ineffable sum of its twists and turns. And his breath trapped inside it.

Group Photos

Out my window there is a *murder* of crows in the trees. They drift like dark dishrags from branch to branch. A *disarray* of metaphors misappropriates the page – they can do that when they are not carefully watched. A *felicity* of ghost memories dances in wet cement and I can only hope they'll get out in time, because there is a *currency* of nows eager to get started. There is a *gallop* of caffeine Annie has lined up at the starting gate. There is a *squint* of sunrays highlighting an *escape* of toast crumbs on the kitchen table, as Annie dips a butter knife into a jar of jam, looks up at me and smiles, says: "You're overthinking things again, aren't you?"

Fire Walker

He'd taken a fire walking workshop in the desert. And now he lay in the ER with his feet bandaged, listening to the guy behind the curtain separating them. To a man's frenzied pleas to have the toilet seat removed (which was Krazy Glued, ambush-style, to his butt by his drug-addled son). He looked down at those traitorous feet, thinking, what a colossal loser he was for not having the *faith* (or imaging he could) to walk over those red embers like the others. How mortifying it was when they had to drive him in, and his screams – Christ – the screams, his biggest declaration of failure. Just like his dad always confirmed when he didn't toe the line, or screwed up because of it. Wished he could have Krazy Glued *him* to the seat – his throne – with his newspaper and magazine rack never out of reach. The candy striper coming in now, all chipper, with a few copies of *People Magazine*, and glancing at those unworthy feet of his with an *Oh-you-poor-thing* look. That sweet face, which had the amazing capacity for shouting: *Loser! Loser!* without ever moving its lips.

The Intruder

My life was finally coming together, and Cassandra was down there waiting for me beside that candy apple red convertible of hers at the landing site. My face was rubberizing in freefall and then the chute blossomed open, and that's when it happened. When the sky said: *Fuck you!* and that bird, a big one, flew in and rose up against the canopy flapping frantically and I could hear its heartbeat against the fabric. No, wait, it was my own, perhaps both. I wanted to prove something to Cassandra/myself by doing this daring stunt and now if that crazy-wild beak kept looking for an exit and tore a hole in my chute the wind pressure would take care of the rest. The creature lowered a bit and I could feel it battering my face, all the hellion things I'd done/what I'd made of my life beating against me. And then, as I cursed it with one last futile scream, it flew out and I could see that hard earth widen, but kept screaming anyway, only now it was different. When I stopped and collected myself, I began directing my chute to the landing zone where that red Caddy, that approving red-lipped smile would be waiting. I decided not to mention anything about the bird.

Reading by Ghost Light

It's astonishing how luminous, how sinewy in recollection their light can be. An ex looms up through the floorboards, brings a horror movie script for me to reread. She scrapes two butter knives together by my ear. An eerie sound effect perhaps. The words blur. An old army buddy glows his way out of a heating duct, a scroll in hand. It's disconcerting because of his low candlepower and the way the scroll keeps curling back into itself, its muscle memory beyond my capacity to tame it. My mother's shimmering ghost memory slips out from behind the drapes, clutching a menu. There is the scent of cigarettes and oven grease. The text is in hieroglyphic profusion. I recognize a few of the animals. The blue plate special looks a little sketchy. My father, incandescent in a wrinkled blue suit, brings a *Book of Facts* that aren't. Held out in the leather vise of a baseball glove from my youth. The book tells something about the social habits of fast flying insects he's highlighted, or the primary punctuation marks of some arcane dead language of affection. It's hard to tell them apart. I turn the page. The small wind it creates, blows out all the lightbulbs.

How Onomatopoeia Saved Their Marriage

"*Kaboom!*" he said, as he poured himself a cup of coffee, wiping goop from his eyes. As their old cat slowly walked by they both looked down and said: "*whoosh!*" then laughed. They were retired now and found themselves looking at the junk mail with interest when it came through the slot in the door, landing softly onto the rug, and he bellowed: "*clunk!*" Later in the day they sat on the couch and watched a fly circle the room. When it landed on a gladiola in a vase, the wife exclaimed: "*boing!*" and he gave a thumbs up. They spent their day expressing themselves in this fashion, with ignited verbiage for the dullest doings. When it came time for bed, notwithstanding the two of them yawning prodigiously, he reached a slow hand under the covers and said: "*bam!*"

From a Diary of a Young House Cleaner

"It was such a pretty little ring and there were so many and the drawer was full of them in all those fancy boxes. Enough for a hundred fingers and who could miss such a little thing? And I am sure it didn't fit anymore anyway. All those chubby fingers must have been skinny once like mine. So it was a shame to leave it there, sad even and I can tell you it is very happy now in its new home for here I have so little and it can feel important and it looks so good on my finger right where it belongs and I will clean all those dusty places in her house she never notices and I never touched cause I think that is fair and a good deal. Maybe even more than fair cause that's just me cause that's just who I am."

Viva Las Vegas

The sky shook the plane out of its hair. It is big enough to do such a thing. There was a fruit picker onboard who used stilts to reach the highest branches and had a saved up wad of cash with which he sought to pick the roulette tables clean. There was an Elvis impersonator with a wig and several glittery jumpsuits in his luggage, and Molly Glum, who was far from it, so eager to drain the casinos of their coffers with her Blackjack skills. Molly so pumped up and spring-loaded, wearing her lucky shoes, shiny as she felt. So happy she just made the flight, barely, racing to her seat beside Elvis, who wasn't Elvis yet and didn't have the voice, the charm, or that lopsided cocky grin, but was sure he would soon enough, channeling "The King." Who offered her his window seat which she took gladly and would later regret as the hard earth rose up at them and everybody screamed except Elvis who just thought, *fuck! – there goes my big shot at being someone, kingly.* And, *fuck, fuck, fuck, wouldn't you just know it!*

An Introduction to Grace

She was a *Prima Ballerina Assoluta* on a cruise ship giving lessons to middle-aged women who sought to recapture long ago capsized longings for grace, and some time away from their husbands. She told me she wanted to be a gazelle in public, and a grunting beast in bed. But really couldn't quite pull off the latter and brought that elegance to the sheets and wrinkled them with refinement. She told me how she had danced with Baryshnikov. How his leaps were like flying and there was that swan's glide to the way she reached for her drink. She was years older than I was back then, but the way she carried herself could give a regal dignity to a folding chair just by the way she sat in it. I read her a poem I'd written about the sea and something about a lacy foam. Told her how I wrote like Baryshnikov and danced like Dostoevsky, and she liked that.

A Rush of Shadows

She fell in with some bad nuns who smoked pot behind the rectory. The eldest had a past, a prison tattoo: the name *Emma* in a heart cracked down the middle under her robes. The other stuttered and cursed herself for doing so. Said the high point of her life was going up all those stairs in the Statue of Liberty as a kid, and looking out from the big lady's crown. Her little eyes above those big ones. Both heads in the clouds. After a jet made a grey scar above them and it was quiet again, the nun with the tattoo said: "Inexhaustible abundance is a myth. You'd be wise to remember that." The novice nodded, watched some fast moving clouds send a rush of shadows across a half-painted house in the distance. Wondered who the hell Emma was.

Trigger Finger

He was a sniper back from the war. A good one. He used that finger now, that steady slow-squeeze finger to turn the pages of the books he always wanted to read, get lost in: classics. Sometimes he'd wet it gently against the tip of his tongue to turn a page when he felt it had gotten too smooth and dry. When he was a kid he had a car door close on a finger, but not that one, and the nail turned black. Sometimes when his mind rolled backwards like a car with no breaks down a hill, he thought of that trigger finger, in historical terms, and wished its entirety blacken to serve as a marker. But when he turned the pages of thick books, it was just the right color. So utilitarian, so ordinary, one could forget (even he) and might not ever know the difference.

The Rapture Workout Video

You visit your best friend and he tells you his older sister has gone to the dark side. That she is a born again Christian fanatic. She is in front of the TV in leotards exercising to *The Rapture* workout video where the instructor is saying: "Now swing those arms and Devil-punch – one, two..." He says she has a tumor-sniffing dog that sniffed her left breast so insistently she went in to have it checked and they found the teeniest something-or-other, but now she's okay. Her dog stares at you as you go into your friend's room to smoke pot like you always do after school and you hope it won't race over and sniff your nuts, or anywhere else for that matter. You think his sister is hot, that you could fight off as many devils as she wants just for one quick feel. Your friend has 3-D comic books and these paper color-tinted glasses and wants to show you how the superheroes leap right off the page. But you are testosterone-severe and, notwithstanding that x-ray-nostriled beast from hell at the ready, eager to fight off demons, kung fu the shit out of them, do whatever it takes.

Impeccable Figure Fours

My father took my mom and me ice skating in the mud. He said figure eights were much too easy and proclaimed he was creating impeccable figure fours only he could perform. Mom's dress got splattered but Dad said it was fine, that now it was a polka-dotted outfit, and *that* was in fashion. At night Mom and I looked out the window up at the sky. Mom said she was searching for "intergalactic vistas" which sounded like a foreign language at the time. Dad was on the couch belching beer ghosts at the TV. We were very poor back then and Mom and I passed a cardboard toilet paper tube back and forth to peer through, to see what might be found beyond it.

Diversity Takes, What We Can Only Hope, Is a Vacation

As far as anyone can tell, it starts with each snowflake exactly alike and then people's noses become the same size and shape. Next: every facial feature/body type/color is identical. The same mole on every left shoulder and everyone speaks the same language down to the pitch and cadence so we look to the sky for answers, wonder if this is some perverse form of entertainment for the gods and if revelations will follow; silence is a hammer swinging down. People no longer have affairs – what for? Folks try to speak in made-up tongues, but can't. Poets write all the same poems and memorize, recite them ad nauseam. Every house and apartment is equal in every detail and there is no jealousy, there is no particular pride. Ambition flatlines. Costume shops are flooded. People enter them with reverence as though entering a cathedral: masks are sold by the pound and we all have the same names: "Dick" and "Jane." Dick jokes go quickly out of fashion and there is only one season: Spring, one species of bird: red-breasted meadowlarks. Its song is a record skipping. Jane and I make love, while I wear a red clown nose, she a purple; all the more elaborate stuff is sold out. We have pages from the *Kamasutra* taped to the walls. Every conceivable sexual position; they are miracles of bodily mechanics we attempt, but it makes no difference. It is always "missionary style."

Feng Shui

She tries to arrange the furniture for the best possible outcomes, but still keeps meeting the same abominable clowns on dating sites no matter where they sit or which way the bed is pointing – the sum of those various parts out of balance. "I want to open up a parachute concession in Heaven when I depart," Long Fingers says, and she thinks: *What the fuck?* Diamond Earring tells her that his ex said he should stick his head in a bucket of grace. That it might do him some good, and she can tell his ex-wife still lives in his timbers like termites. Perfect Teeth tells her most women he meets act like he has a solid gold skeleton inside him they can't wait to excavate. That they are always trying so hard to get inside him, "deep," he says – "you know?" When he is in the bathroom she turns the chair he was sitting in around to face the wall. Finally, alone, she decides it doesn't matter which way the furniture is facing and sits with the cat and a glass of wine by the window and listens to the soothing *slishh* of passing traffic in the rain. The cat, the wine, the traffic all facing in the right direction.

Exterminator

By day I'm a hitman. But in the evenings I go to homes for the aged and read to the blind. All day I visit apartments and houses with my implements of death. Drive a small truck with a large plastic bug on its roof which looks somewhat extraterrestrial. Moby Dick (I don't care how long it takes) is a favorite and nothing scurries or crawls into cracks. And I'm not the one with the thirst for killing. I love to watch those dead eyes light up at the sound of my voice. It brightens some fractured dark inside of me. And those quirky human-interest pieces from the papers I read aloud are a big hit too: The man who beat a burglar half to death with his prosthetic leg, and the... As a kid my dad would always shut me up, found zippers for my words, as my mom looked away to count the wallpaper roses. But now I can be Ahab bellowing, fierce-toned and welcomed. And as for the rats and roaches, well, they had better watch their step.

Bug Porn

Curled over the microscope, he was watching cells divide in a harsh moon of light. *What are you up to?* she asked. She had come down the short flight of stairs, wearing a lacy red bra over her blouse. Just to be silly. To see where it might go. *Watching bug porn*, he said, with one eye squinted shut. When he opened it and looked at her, he shook his head Jotted something in a notebook. They were in the basement where he had his office, and she noticed a daddy longlegs above them on the low ceiling. Thought, how stunningly elegant it was; that tiny body ambling on slender threads. When she pointed it out, he stood quickly and swung his notebook, smashing it just inches from the light bulb. *Bug porn*, she said after a pause, and could see he was pleased that she had registered his little joke. She reached back and unhooked her bra. Flung it over her shoulder; a dangling epaulet. Gazed up at the single leg stuck to the ceiling. Angled, just so, like a forward slash. With all of the surrounding grammar missing.

The Drawer

It was a top drawer in an old maple desk and it was locked. Their father had left them years before it happened, and it had happened way too soon. Now there was this house and all that was in it for the two sisters (her daughters) to roam through like a high-hedged maze, hoping for an exit. The one sister thought jewels were in the drawer, gold perhaps, a stack or two of large denominational bills. And the other imagined love letters their father had sent her, years before they were born (bound by a rubber band that parted into a dried worm when you touched it). The key to the drawer was in the pocket of a frayed housedress draped over a chair in the well of the desk. When one of the sisters grabbed the garment to toss, she felt it. There was nothing spoken between them as they gaped into the open drawer at the collection of sex toys (in an unthinkably wide range of colors and sizes – *oh, my god!*) and they shut it quickly, deciding they'd done enough for one day and left. Bent and huddled together under one of their mother's old umbrellas, comforted under the taut, dull fabric out into the rain.

Grizzly

He sat with his naked feet in the baby pool, a rifle on his lap, and waited for the bear. His wife loved animals (all the way down to the insect kingdom – most of it) and they'd argued over whether or not to shoot it. When she offered to put food out for it, saying the "poor thing" was just hungry, that's when he got out his gun. Their kids were grown with kids of their own and the little rubberized baby pool with the seahorses on it was a relic he pulled from the shed. It was the fourth day of triple-digit heat and Lilly figured what the hell, she might as well join him since the bear was no dummy and wasn't going to come around with him sitting there with that cannon on his lap. She brought some more ice cubes to add to the pool water and her guitar and her own bare feet and sweet singing voice. And despite himself, though he still was a bit miffed, he sang along.

Metaphors Incognito

Metaphors feel ill-attended, disabused, go into hiding. Or wear strange disguises: bushy opera beards and clumpy steel-toe boots, even the most ethereal of them. They stand by vacant storefronts in killer bee costumes, pretend not to be what they are and discuss the world with esoteric banter. Some poets go mad, their minds spinning like dust devils in the vacuum and count the crumbs at the bottom of their toasters with stale words on their tongues. Other poets sit in diners and mistake the tines of forks for musical instruments they cannot play. A particularly stunning metaphor drives a convertible along the coast, the wind making a horizontal freedom flag of its long wig, and will not be had at any price. At night one metaphor says to another: "Longing is a beggar that bites," and the other replies: "And fire is fond of sharing its rubies." They titter for a moment, then slink unceremoniously into the dark maw of the woods.

The Polygamist's Three Wives

The commune stood between a vast stretch of scrub oaks. A land purring with haiku, few noticed. The three women sat in the kitchen around a pie one of them had baked. Realized each of them had been faking orgasms. The youngest one blushed. The middle wife was suddenly taken with the blades of the ceiling fan. The eldest, spit out a bit of pie as she laughed, which the baby on her lap stabbed with a finger and ate. He sat in the next room. Looked over imperiously, and smiled. He was playing chess with his oldest, and not knowing which piece to move, he moved his coffee cup from one coffee ring to another. Off the kitchen, was the clomping sound of sneakers jogging around in the dryer, mixed with the wives' laughter. A bee flew in one window and out another, preferring the roses.

Dancing with Wolves

We drove to the edge of the forest under a hunter's moon where the wolves were waiting. We'd met online at: *NoStringsAndUpForSomethingWild.com*, and she was even prettier in 3-D. The wolves were nose-up howling and performing their elaborate and snarly movements as we mimicked them, howling too. With wide seductive eyes on each other, and a Super-Glued peripheral vision on the beasts. "This is *so* damn exciting," she said, and that she liked the way the moonlight glistened off their canines. I leaned in close and asked if she knew that gray wolves mated for life, and she gazed at me with an intermittent and penetrating mix of direct and askance vision and stopped dancing. Headed for the road where we parked the car. As I followed, it suddenly got darker, the moon buttering a bank of clouds and coaxing an uneasy silence behind me as the howling ceased.

Leo the Leviathan

His real name was Ben, but he was *Leo the Leviathan* in the ring. Wore a costume of fake seaweed, like endless green tassels and a plethora of stick-on barnacles. Even on his face. Begging her on his cell, in whispers, to reconsider. To take him back. His *Oh, baby, please baby* – coming out: *Uh-huh...uh-huh...* The phone so tiny in that big scaly hand. And when she hung up on him, he wanted to weep. An ocean's worth. But Cyclops Cid, with his black eyepatch up over his head, was going through his locker across from him, looking for that talking turtle picture book his daughter wanted him to read. And besides, leviathans were not supposed to have tear ducts. Any *decent*, true-blooded leviathan that is.

War and My Father at the Kitchen Table

War blasts in through the screen door and sits at our kitchen table fingering the butcher knives. My father sits across from it smoking a *Lucky*, not at all feeling so. War breaks out a deck of cards and they play, War looking for "tells" and my father looking for recompense. My father never mentions War, but I have often seen it on his shoulders as he sulked about, with War's hairy fingers laced across his eyes. "Ante up," War says, "it'll put hair on your balls," and my father glares at it without moving, so still his unlucky *Lucky* is nearly all ash. A large bird flies in through the open window and brushes past the stubble on War's face and is set ablaze. "Excellent!" War says and slaps the table, "we eat!"

Fixed Forms

When I asked about the latest guy she was seeing, she told me there were times when it was like glimpsing a fin circling just above the surface and how absurd that seemed. But wondered, nonetheless, if there was a shark attached. Said that in the quiet moments after sex how loudly his tattoos spoke to her. Not "spoke" spoke of course, but spoke of what he'd hidden under all that cotton. I told her I had my own version with the women I was dating. How sometimes it was like trying to keep an eye out for bees in a snowstorm, and how many times we'd both been stung. "This is sounding weird and paranoid," she said, and she was right. We'd been friends since childhood and being each other's reliable confidants and counselors had replaced *much* else, so she asked me how my back was feeling and I asked about her knee as our eyes locked for a moment, then looked away.

Visitation

Afirefly glided in through the open window with its little lantern and circled Cassie. She looked up from the book she was reading and her mouth swung open, but nothing came out. "What?" I said, seeing something happening to her face. The creature's little light was blinking and Cassie followed its orbit with rapt adherence and I said, "What?" again, watching it too, that meager touch of grace with a tiny flickering moon in it. "Mom?" she said, and I wondered if I should close the window to extend the moment she was having, whatever that was, but the little thing flew out into the night taking Cassie's mixtures with it. I got up and shut the window. *Hey, it's just a bug,* I thought, saw a bit of wind in the chimes, suddenly aware that a window knows two seasons. I turned and entered ours.

Superhero

I do not have a superpower. But an uncanny ability to finish sentences. This, of course, does not translate to crime fighting; swinging from a spidery thread up or down a skyscraper. But flinging, instead, the populous at the *Peaceful Willow* rest home into a state of awe and wonder. Prying loose pieces of syntax from the rubble. The names of favorite shows and presidents, trapped in walls; particles of plaster trickling down as they strain to think. *Tapioca*, I tell Mrs. Green, trying to describe what otherwise translates, descriptively, as "mud". Nobody's thinking I'm a bird, a plane; faster than a speeding bullet. Yet I see through walls. *Your Uncle, Jake*, I say to another. *The tall one with the nice smile. That who?* And: *You mean, Rose Sunset? That pretty rouge you wear? Tyrone Power… Epson salts… Chrysanthemums…* I say. *You're certainly welcome. Close*, I say. *But, it's Roy. Oh, hon*, I say, *think nothing of it.*

so much depends...

We sat on a couch for wallflowers who sipped their drinks. She struck me as old-fashioned. Like she would have ridden a bicycle sidesaddle if she could. Outside, a blizzard banged at the windows. I told her I was a writer. She said, "Who isn't"? That she had a cousin who made up names for rodeo bulls. *Chicken on a Chain* was one. Said: "He writes". The crowd thinned and took much of the body heat with them. She pulled out a joint. Asked what I wrote. When I said poetry, she said, 'Who doesn't." We smoked it to the nub and went into the kitchen. Put our hands over the red coils of a toaster. Smiling when they touched. She told me she had a favorite poem tattooed to her left cheek. Would I like to see it? I nodded. She lifted her dress, tugged at her panties. And there it was: Williams Carlos Williams' "The Red Wheelbarrow." In Courier. Like it was typed there. I was buzzed and the image of the red wheelbarrow and the white chickens seemed so basic, so necessary to me. "Your turn," she said, putting herself back together, and our hands rose up again. I considered what it was I had to offer. Gazed out at a landscape losing its color. A snowman gaining way too much weight.

Bomb Shelter

I could almost feel my father's curious disappointment that it never happened. That searing and disintegrating light he never had a chance to mitigate with his preparedness. Those drab green cans of stacked water, rations: his and our salvation that never came to pass. The atomic realization later, that anticipated things that do not occur can steer a life with hot hands on the wheel. The atomic blasts which arrived, were *so* ordinary: bills, the bottle, the piled up weight of days. Weeds now atop that subterranean vault. A stack of *Better Homes & Gardens* rotting in a corner, a rusted out transistor radio that never did, but should have, with staticky panic told him/us how wise, how very, very wise he'd been.

Mr. and Mrs. God

Mrs. God told Mr. God, peering down at the wounded multitudes, that *scars were screaming mouths zipped shut*. Mr. God was in a mischievous mood inventing something. He was always inventing something. Told Her She thought too much and was reading too much crappy poetry. Mrs. God told Him that He wasn't the only one with lofty notions, that Her brain was big as His, and She wanted to start an "advice column" in answer to the many prayers of the misbegotten. "What?" Mr. God said, looking up from the screechy, bile-spewing thing He was tinkering with. "Don't go messing with the order of things," He cautioned. "It's *perfected,* and the silence they receive from me is something they can twist into any shape they choose – it works like a charm." Then, in that momentary distraction, Mr. God said, "Shit!" and began sucking a bloody finger. "The damn thing bit me."

Saw Blade

I talk Nina into it; Ed goes along. Neither can figure why I'm still pining over Rita. The three of us have a musical saw band. Pass the hat most times. Carry around these small collapsible garden seats. Sit under Rita's window, the saws between our knees, bending and bowing Rita's favorite: *Head Like a Hole.* Her window's open and I'm hoping she'll find the sorrowful tones, the sweet sentiment, irresistible. But I'm beginning to think she's not home, till it starts raining some of my paperbacks. Troopers that we are, we keep playing. One by one they're flying out. And then this shirtless guy with a plethora of angry animal tattoos sticks his head out, says, "Get lost you crazy fucks!" as a hand snakes around his waist and eases him back in. The fingernails painted *Cayenne Pepper Red*. Rita's favorite go-to shade. We stop and Nina picks up one of the books, coos: "*Baudelaire*. Can I have it?" I nod and we pack up. *Los Guanacos* is a couple of streets down and if the mariachis aren't there, we've got a spot. Nina looks at me as we head off, Baudelaire in a reverential clutch. "Nothing like a saw," she says, "to cut through all the bullshit."

How to Fit an Elephant in Your Heart

The thing to remember is how elastic that ticking framework is. But one mustn't take liberties either. The small pile of hay will come first as an inducement. Clear the room of any "breakables." Next replace the washers in your eye-faucets to avoid leakage. A slippery entry is to be avoided. Take a deep satisfying breath. The incision should be clean, straight, and long. Keep a roll of Scotch tape handy. Additionally, keep a bottle of alcoholic spirits nearby. The beast may need a shove or two. I wish I could tell you there's something to be done about the tusks, but hey, that's all part of the deal, isn't it? When that last foot is in, tape quickly. A crisscross pattern is advised. Double up. Breathe. Pour a glass, or drink straight from the bottle. Kick back and wait for the call/text/email you know is never coming. Adjust to the additional poundage. It may take a while. That is of no particular concern, and is precisely as it should be.

Gravity's Big Hands

It was another hair-brained dream session and he told me all he needed was his camera and a ticket to Hollywood. He reminded me of a bird that kept crashing into windows, seeing everything but the pane. He was planning on being what he called "a paparazzi" like it was a royal title and that he was going to take nude photos of famous actresses and sell them for millions, and of course it was about as likely he would leave as drive to Mars for the weekend. But coughing out dreams along with our marijuana smoke was a way to pass the time back then and a way to forget he was working at Safeway bagging other people's weight gain. My dream came out in a smooth stream of smoke that I could somehow do a magic trick with those 26 mystical letters in the English alphabet, put into a top hat, mix them with my magic wand and pull out books of my poetry. One after another to deafening applause. When the joint was down to a tiny roach he took out a little tin box and added it to a colony of them. Then we both just stared out over the town from that hilltop as a few pigeons in the distance flew off in a frenzy from a church bell tower once the bell began to ring.

Leaning In

They stripped for each other on Zoom, and he did a simulated drum cymbals accompaniment with his tongue against his teeth, as she tossed her bra, a bit of spittle shooting out. The years hadn't been particularly kind. But they *oohed* and *aahed* nonetheless. Later, with their clothes back on, leaning in so close to the screen their faces coned, they talked about their grown children. How, with his young daughter on his shoulders once at the circus, the man on stilts reached down to shake her hand. How she squealed through the magic. How he wished he had that photo. She told of her ex-husband's obsession with huge cars. Especially Cadillacs. Their kids as props beside them. How he kept stepping back and back with his Polaroid, trying to fit them in, till the kids were nearly smudges – door handle-sized against them. Albums full. "Wow," he said. When the talk waned, they stretched out the cords of their computer cameras and showed each other the natural light that pushed in through their respective windows. Thousands of miles apart. His light was a bit sunnier than her own. Her window, blocked somewhat by a fat cat and a stained glass fish dangling from the frame. There were streaks on his pane where rain had run down through the dust she'd never see. "Here, kitty- kitty," he said, pointing past her. Leaning in even closer, misunderstanding, she said, "*Meow.*"

Close Calls

He collected dented breastplates from centuries old battles. They were up on the walls in his den and I couldn't help but wonder if he'd gotten them cheaper that way, being damaged and all. "Oh, no," he told me, as we passed a joint back and forth as though we were underwater and sharing a mouthpiece to a single tank of air. "It's a reminder is all, of close calls: a battle-axe, an arrow that never got its appetite appeased." He had an eyepatch over one eye which I never asked about, and as the marijuana stormed the barricades, I viewed those wall hangings with fresh eyes. Thought of all the swords that nearly made it through, so easily forgotten and how it's the deep splinters and the mosquito's sly insertion that drive one mad. How the critical close calls are good for chitchat and a nervous laugh, then, "Hey, what's for dinner?" There was one on the wall with a deep gash above the place a heart would beat with that fierce banging on either side of the plate, and as I marveled, I could feel that one good eye on me.

Interpreter of Dreams

My mother was the self-appointed interpreter of dreams, coughing out her verdicts with an early morning smoke. Mining her slumber for forecasts in a flourish of recitations: silverware meant guests were coming – hands: a gift; bees represented bad luck (especially if they were swarming), and "teeth," the one we dreaded most, meant *certain death*. And it didn't matter whose: a family member, a neighbor, even old celebrities counted, were not safe, and we'd wait for the ax to fall, and of course, it always did and she'd say: *See!* The Rosetta Stone she carried in her head, infallible back then. Her catalog of icons: keys to the future. As we listened with our spoons frozen over cold bowls of cereal. She, in her robe, with her coffee and her cigarettes and the fate of the world in her hands.

Email from a Starry-Eyed Desk Clerk Working at a Cheap Hotel

"I'm blowing it Hank and you know how I've always kept a safe distance had my fun but never let anyone "in" where they might do some damage. Well, get this, I've fallen for one of the local hookers that comes here with her johns and sometimes she stops by "after" and we talk and have these great conversations and believe me when I tell you she's got an opinion on just about everything and she's a straight shooter like you and me and fuck if I haven't fallen for her and in the sack it's the real deal. No faking it I can tell and we've even been to the movies like a regular couple. There's juice, Hank and I know that sounds corny, especially to your ears because you know me so well but shit's changed and hey, what's the use of being in a bulletproof car if you keep all the windows open, right? But hell I couldn't help it, and now I've gotta watch her take the elevator with some slob who doesn't know who the hell she is or how much she's really worth – Christ! We need to get soused and talk and soon and maybe you can make some sense of it. Her street name is Mink, Mandy Mink like the ritzy fur but everybody calls her Mink for short. But her real name is Susan."

Fatherly Advice in a Letter from a Drunken Poet

"P.S. Just remember, son, keep a keen eye out for those "crimes of juxtaposition" – you know: *this* too close to *that*, because they can be tricky, treacherously so.

P.P.S. Calamities' au pairs are waiting in line around the block looking for work. RUN!

P.P.P.S. It is well worth keeping in mind, a parachute is a brake that can fly, and this might come in handy, if only for a critical moment.

P.P.P.P.S. And never forget: each morning is an ode to mobility, and mobility is an ode to quest. We are not trees, are not stitched to this earth. *Shoes, shoes* – thank god for them!"

Ways to View and Categorize Mirages

Wear someone else's glasses (the stronger their prescription the better) and keep your distance. Distance is a wedding ceremony for a mirage, but there will not be a honeymoon. Yet still you can blow wet kisses from afar. Mirages can be real as tattoos, as colorful, as painful to remove. I lived with a mirage once. Didn't keep my distance; she had a name that rhymed with *daylight*: not the word, but the phenomenon. I could touch her even in the shower, she was that real and the water beaded on her skin. Who could know? I wore my uncle's glasses: the frames were thick and black and the lenses made my eyes owlish as he told me stories of the mirages he'd categorized, tattooed all the way up his arm (a tattoo "X" through each). When mine vanished like wind-blown mist, her name rhymed with *intangible*. Not the phenomenon, but the word.

The Lion's Cage

I visit my ex in the lion's cage. The lion is asleep and I talk in whispers, but she speaks full-throated. It is her lion after all, her cage, ostensibly. She asks how I'm doing as I retrieve a small box of my books and a waffle iron that was a wedding gift she no longer wants. And tell her how: uncertainty flies with one wing and its head turned backwards and that there is no telling where or when it will roost. No, wait, actually I say: "Fine – I'm doing fine." The lion twitches in its slumber, its claws flaring (no doubt reddening something with slower legs) and for a moment I recall how sweet the waffles tasted, dripping syrup onto those cheap plates we had back then. "Well, I guess that's it," I say. There are two cage bars wider apart than the rest she directs me to, with a finger to her lips, and shows me the new way out.

The Hypnotist in Retirement

She told him she played connect-the-dots in her head with the gopher holes in the park. Saw something *unimaginable*. He never asked. But he always listened and looked up from whatever he was doing. When she asked if he ever missed working the clubs, he'd tell her he didn't. Just detaching from a 1,000-piece jigsaw puzzle or those shifting rows of cards as he played solitaire. Every so often she struggled to dispel the notion that he had her hop like a bunny or quack like a duck during the quiet hours when she couldn't feel him there.

The Short Happy Life of Uncle Sal

They were everywhere, anywhere my Aunt Rose couldn't find them. Those nudist magazines slid under old tires and boards. Sun-bright women playing ping-pong and tug-of-war in the buff. My Uncle Sal digging them out of garage clutter. My young eyes bugging out as he slipped one under my shirt and patted it. The stink-eye my Aunt Rose gave back at the house. The runes she read as I stared down at my shoes. The cookies she gave me anyway. The daggers he got as he headed to the fridge for a beer. Uncle Sal, who worked in a tire plant and joked, he always had a *big roll*. Dead on the can at 34; an artery in his chest exploding like a bottle under a truck backing up. Slumped over. "Never made a peep," my Aunt said. "Not a peep." Years later, marrying a religious man who didn't drink and never made a peep either. The huge Nativity scene he put out each year lighting up half the neighborhood. One of the Three Wise Men looking eerily like Uncle Sal, without the beard of course, who'd be toting a stack of *Sun-Baked Babes,* had it been, I imagined, instead of frankincense or myrrh.

Evolution in Sloth-Time

I prayed to a god with three front teeth missing and one black eye. Figured lowering my expectations would be a safe bet. But it never did work out, because I found myself, an expert diamond cutter, chipping away at beach glass washed, willy-nilly, ashore. It was at that time I met Laura, who was knitting sweaters for her seven cats which even on the coldest days kept them running in circles and biting at the yarn. So my prayers were sort of answered. On the night my god visited me his head was bandaged and one arm was in a sling and he drooled, told me: "Hey, you ain't seen nothing yet – keep them cards and letters coming." When Laura told me she was cutting a record album of divine music by setting off rat traps at precise intervals, I prayed to a different god who had accidentally Super Glued his fingers together, but recited the haiku of Bashō with amazing resonant pauses. We take the good with the bad, don't we? – and there's much to be said for that.

This Weather We're Having

The left side of our house blew off. We had a spare room there and a canary we can only hope got out somehow safely and flew away. We found the empty cage in ruin. Holly, wrapped in a blanket (it was hot enough to fry your lungs a month ago) comes in with a pot of tea and a battered book of haiku and reads me one to wrestle a small bit of comfort from this moment. "You kindle the fire," she reads, "and I'll show you something wonderful – a big ball of snow." "Nice," I tell her as she shares the blanket and we gaze out the window. There's a piano on fire in the snow and our neighbors around it rubbing their hands together, and we can hear that they are singing, their voices frosting out, but for the life of us we can't tell what or why.

One-and-Only

I ride bucking broncs on the rodeo circuit. The bones in me forget their place sometimes and, with a little encouragement, go their separate ways. Asia, my latest one-and-only, wants me to quit and sell swimming pools for a living instead, because it gets pretty hot here and she says we'd be swimming in cash, then laughs at her own joke, which is not really a joke. She does that a lot. She keeps getting me Hawaiian shirts which make me look like some fancy flower garden, tells me it "softens" me, but I don't want to be softened. I've got a second one-and-only on the other side of town who goes to all my events and sees right through me to that beat-up skeleton deep in there and thinks it's kind of noble. Her word. And she hates the Hawaiian shirts and said if I ever wore one around her again she'd take a pair of garden sheers to them, and we both got a good laugh out of that one. She's alright that particular one-and-only.

The Flying Blunders

My mother drove a steamroller around the house for a time, thinking that might work. There were a lot of inglorious things popping up my mother wished to flatten. But said it was fatiguing and bad for the furniture, and my father, looking up from TV news agreed. So that's when they joined the circus as a trapeze act: *The Flying Blunders*, hoping an aerial union might be the ticket. Mom would do a triple flip nearly grazing the tent top and wait for my father to catch her as he hung from the bar by his knees reading the newspaper. But gravity took more interest and the safety net became her truest lover (as the crowd gasped) she'd tell me all those years later living alone. "It was always there," she'd say: "reliable. Waiting to catch me in its arms."

The Man of the House

My dad lived in a dollhouse for a time after he left us. He bragged that he didn't need any nutty-pills like Alice in Wonderland either, that that was cheating. His legs burst out of the first floor windows as he paced about like a hermit crab, his head through the roof; the chimney for a hat. The miniature table and chairs kept sliding against the papered walls, the tiny kitchen stove, he complained, kept hitting him in the nuts. "Why not get a bigger place?" I asked. "I always was a *homebody*," he told me and laughed at that corny joke he was saving up. He puffed on the stub of what was once a long Cuban cigar, waved a bit sheepishly, then withdrew like a tortoise. And I could hear that teeny, barely audible TV click on. He'd always wanted to feel like a big man in a world where true proportions didn't favor him. And now he'd finally pulled it off.

Reclamation

I told her if I were God, I would have handed out personal-ized manuals for what to expect from this life, as we sat on the blanket, sand-basted. "Well, you're not, and there aren't any, so get over it," she told me as we watched the sea swine grunting their way toward shore. The barnacled rhinos lumbered dangerously close, but we passed sunscreen back and forth pre-tending not to notice. Sighing, she rolled over, undid her bikini top and vanished into a novel like a magic trick. I reached in the ice chest and grabbed a cold one, trying not to pay atten-tion to something slithery wriggling by just beneath the sand. Disappearing was not my specialty, but creating small gulping waterfalls of alcoholic beverages down my gullet was, and that would just have to do.

Origami Monsters

She never wants to talk things out, has a period at the beginning of every sentence. Makes origami monsters when she's pissed and leaves them in a bowl on the coffee table, then goes in her room and turns her music up to where the windows rattle. These teenage years are an alphabet soup for us with all the vowels missing. She tells her mother and myself she wants to start a musical spoons band with a couple of her friends from school and we're thrilled. Hey, if flatware can be a conduit for expression we're all for it, and we listen to her practice in her room. When she gets a boyfriend with creepy tattoos and a too-loud motorcycle, she leaves origami swans and cranes for us, and the silverware returns. When my wife and I have soup we sip it slowly, glance up. Aware the spoons will never be the same.

The Butcher's Long-Winded Goodbye Note

"For the record you've always been a cut above and a good cut is something I know a thing or two about but I've never been the kind of guy who could be housebroken and I don't mean like a dog or cat probably more like a wild stallion. But ever since I moved into your place you've tried to tame me had me smoke outside regardless of the weather and you knew how much I loved that wiggly hula dancer lamp of mine God the kicks I got out of that thing when I wound her up and when you banished her to the garage it broke my heart. Well now she's in the back of my truck safe and sound and I know how much you like to talk things out till you're blue in the face but my mind's made up. Whatever I've left behind you can keep or sell but please dump that toaster my dad left me cause one of these days it's just gonna go up in flames and as far as the fish tank I couldn't take with me, please don't overfeed my darlings cause a little dash'll do. Hell I'm sure gonna miss them little guys and the peaceful sound those bubbles made at night when you were beside me sawing logs and I had a chance to sneak in a few puffs. I'm really gonna miss them too."

In Lieu of Birdsong

Each day Brad fired a small cannon from his backyard just to watch the songbirds in his neighbor's tree tear for the heavens. There was no good reason, he thought, why the birds hadn't initially fluffed out his own tree with song but determined it might be the cheerful laughter of his neighbor, Ralph, and his trophy wife that drew the birds; a kind of musical kinship – *Christ, some people!* Of course how could any of them know that Brad was a general on the battlefield at all the Civil War reenactments, a gentleman of stature and command and had the wiry burnsides facial hair to prove it. He hovered over the fuse now with a cigarette lighter his father had given him when his dad was only a private in the war and couldn't beat the women off. Brad knew all the stories as a Biblical scholar might. When the fuse sparked, his dog, "Bugle Boy" ran into the house, and for only one short moment longer, there'd be that sweet music in someone else's leaves.

Never an Endangered Species

I see a man sitting on a park bench beside an old coffee maker, think of the possibilities: (A) It was there before he sat down, (B) He was kicked out of his place and this was all he could think to take, and (C) He brought it along simply because it was better than an empty space beside him. There are, after all, these infernal spaces to fill, but the good news is, he is not talking to it, and the better news is, it is not talking back. Loneliness, I consider, will never be an endangered species. The rest of the long walk home is uneventful. When I reach the top of the landing in my apartment building that changes, as I see a lovely woman wearing a babushka milking a goat. The sound of the milk striking the side of the pail is a kind of reliable melody in contrast to the erratic whoosh and honk from the traffic below. I put my key in the lock – "Thank you, Rita," I tell her without turning, pausing only to listen to it a bit longer.

The Breath as Storm, the Breath as Gentle Breeze

Cynthia gives birth to a *whisper*. Her husband, Gus, is not pleased. "I was hoping for a *shout*," he says. "But it's a boy like you wanted, and he has your eyes." The *whisper* is swaddled in Cynthia's arms. Gus strains to hear its little sounds. "How am I going to watch sports with a *whisper* when he grows up? We need to shout at the TV." Cynthia puts a silencing finger to her lips as the *whisper* drifts off. They drop it. Weeks later Gus wakes from a dream where he and God are in a bar watching the game on TV when God turns and spits in his drink. "Fuck," Gus says. "Some people..." Then he hears it, faintly through the intercom in the baby's room. Cynthia whispering. He strains to make it out. Thinks he hears, "Daddy." Or maybe it's Caddy. He owns one. An ocean liner-long vintage Eldorado. Then he hears: "loudmouth" or is it "proud shout." *Hmm*. Finally, he hears "asshole" in a sinewy tone. He rolls back the covers. Follows his erection to the bathroom for a pee. The rest is up in the air, he concludes. But he's pretty certain about that last part.

Cold Light

He was a sewer worker. Was old enough to remember Ed Norton from *The Honeymooners* being one. All the ribbing he took because of it. So he said he worked for the Water Department. Was beginning to date again. Went to a restaurant where the table candle was battery operated, nearly real-looking. She told him she was a hand model when she was younger, and he noticed how balletic she made them, even with the simplest acts. That now she ran a vacuum cleaner repair shop, and if he said he bet it sucked, she'd crown him. They laughed and he saw she had something leafy between her teeth, but didn't know her well enough to mention it. When there was a snag in the conversation, and those hands danced around the table touching things, lingering, he decided he didn't like the fake candle at all. Not because it wasn't interesting, but that he missed getting close sometimes and feeling the warmth, even the burn of the real thing. The way it moved with the slightest winds; the swing of an arm toward the salt. And that quick-vanishing flick of smoke when you blew it out. He liked that too.

Ledge at the Edge of the World

I pull into a rest stop at the edge of the world. Who knew? My GPS has been acting up for weeks. But who could have anticipated *this*? There are people with their bare feet hanging over the edge, wiggling their toes in outer space. Lovers hugging and gazing out as if at a drive-in movie, families bunched together … All the "wrong turns" people are here, inadvertently brought to this spot where land ends. Is extinct. And there are no horizons. Only the universe to ponder without a road, a field, a mountain to landmark the transition. There is no floor like the Grand Canyon. There is only outer space. That star-bright dappled panoply. A road ending at the edge of all that vastness. *All* roads ending: paths of preconceptions, trails of mollifying knowns … I don't smoke (quit years ago) but go into the lone convenience store at the world's end and buy a pack and a can of beer. Sit on the ledge with the others. No one speaks. It's dark now and there are stars, top and bottom. What else is there between them, other than the black spaces? The cigarette smoke burns my throat. The beer never tasted better. But there is no distraction capable of topping this. No grand notion. No presupposed meanderings. There are lights along the edge. There is an infinity of lights beyond that. I guzzle. Watch the cigarette smoke sail off into the unknown.

Sonic Boom

He looked up and told her that an airplane was like a blister on the heavens. "Get a grip," she said, "this garden isn't going to plant itself." There were two saplings angled against the fence, a wheelbarrow filled with perennials, and he picked the trowel up, plunged it into the soil. *Some personalities were so large they dispersed another's language altogether,* he thought, *left it to languor in the lungs.* She handed him some bulbs – "How deep do you want these holes?" he asked. She demonstrated without speaking, and when she turned, he noticed her shadow filled an empty bucket to the brim.

A Home for Monsters

Betty waltzed in holding the baby monster against her chest. I took one look at it and winced. She told me it wouldn't kill me to show a little good cheer, and how monsters had feelings too. She took the monster everywhere and it soon became too large to carry, so she hired a weightlifter. His name was Hugo and he and the monster enjoyed playing rummy and arm-wrestling on the card table Hugo brought over, which kept tipping and spilling their drinks. When I brought home a monster of my own it was fully grown and clicked in a bit clumsily in red high heels and had electric hair that made little strike marks against the kitchen walls, Betty, no matter how hard she tried, couldn't wash off.

The Translator

When he translates the sea he always excludes any mention of the waves. Especially those high-gripping greedy ones that never give back. They form a syntax too difficult for him to untangle. Storm winds, he translates as zephyrs: exacting a gentle nod from the lilies, a light ting or two from the chimes rising slowly from their slumber. When she packs her bags and scoops up their Chihuahua, Mighty Joe Young, and tells him what a "vacuous creep" he's been (in Biblical text) he jots it all down in translation. Every word, in reconstruction (language to language). Each cultural nuance, context, phrasing – that lingering resonance penetrating the page. So exquisite, so musical. So filled with love.

Devil Logs at the Lake

She said she used to have conjugal visits with the Devil at a local penitentiary, but the past was the past and that's where she buried it. Six feet under. And for me not to pay them tattoos of hers no never mind neither 'cause they didn't mean a frog's ass worth of nothin' anymore. We were at the lake and she just came over to the blanket I was dripping lake water on, dragging her not-so-buried history behind her like fresh cut logs, and the strain of it was deep in her brow. "You got a cigarette?" she said for openers. But I was breathing in all that oxygen from that bank of scrub oaks in a circle around us and shook my head. My wife was still in the lake, treading water and looking over. "The Devil still writes," she said, "but I just ball the dang things up 'cept for the pretty ones with poems in 'em – the Devil sure can sweet talk – ooh-wee!" She ran a chipped purple fingernail up and down her face like it was a match she was trying to strike, said: "Hey, you sure you ain't got a cigarette?"

Philosophical Conversation at the House of Pancakes Between Two "Dudes" Stoned on LSD

Dude one: "You can't approximate infinity, dude.

Dude two: "Hey, think about it, when angels lose their wings, I bet catapults would make up for it, you know, like a way to get around."

Dude one: "I heard angels cover the tops of skyscrapers in braille so the wind can read out loud."

Dude Two: "Cool, but what if we're all just God's graffiti scribbled on a bathroom wall?"

Dude one: "That's so way off, man, graffiti can't eat pancakes."

Dude two: "Thanks, Man."

In Silhouette

The bedroom was dark except for a thin sprinkle of moonlight through the blinds. He stood outside the closed bathroom door, leaning in "My name is Ellasandra," his wife, June, of 23 years, said in an accent which, had it been a dog, would have been a mutt. "You here for long, I mean in this country?" he asked with his own accent between French and Madagascan, his breath against the door as was her own on the other side. "Just long enough for the angels to weep," she said. "Just long enough to sizzle." His breath was nearly burning through the separating panel as he said with a quasi-Texan drawl, "Well darlin', sizzle is ma middle name and my first is so hot the devil cannot speak it." And Ellasandra/Annika/Tangerine opened the door and came out into the dimly lit room and let her robe fall away. They were silhouettes now, living Rorschach tests of each other, were all and everything they needed to be.

Newfound

He brings home the wrong suitcase from the airport. It has a monocle, a black cape, and a book of prestidigitation tinged with dark arts in it. It takes a bit to learn how to keep the monocle in, and a good deal of squinting is required. But the cape is fetching and goes well with his pair of black chinos pants he breaks out. And somehow he feels instantly transformed, powerful and, notwithstanding the pants, a bit aristocratic, as the cat glares at him suspiciously. Though it's a bit blurry, he reads the book of magic through the monocle all day instead of going to work. He learns sleight of hand and how to levitate (kind of) while gravity slinks somewhere out of reach, and when his wife complains, with a wave of his cape, he makes her disappear – well, not really, but yes, really too.

All the People We Have Ever Been

I told her all the secrets of my past had zippers. Told her to just pull at will, that their teeth would unclench. But she got lost in their mazes with weary fingers and the jack-in-the-box quality of them startled her. Secrets too early revealed can be like mammoths with clumsy feet making much of every step. She handed me a crowbar and told me to have at it with a few of her own. "That's all you got?" I told her with sweat dripping, a small cannonball pyramid of them I stacked at my feet. But she just said to give it time, how they all were fond of flying.

Air Story

He told her he played air guitar and began doing so, contorting his face with passionate abandon as he plucked away at oxygen. She said she knew that tune by Hendrix, that it was a favorite. When she began doing air oil painting, it was like nothing he'd ever seen and he felt like a fraud, a copycat. *Hendrix for chrissake!* When the last drop of air oil paint touched the air canvas he sighed. High above them an airplane bulleted through the heavens; all those people going somewhere fast. Just enough to make one wonder.

Zigzaggy

I awake zigzaggy like lightning. Flash through the day that way, charring the rug, lighting sticks of marijuana, fireplaces. My friends are delighted, use me to charge their phones and, when wrapped in dark nights, crave my contrast. I think to join the circus, but *damn*, there aren't any. I join a dating site instead: "Zigzaggy man who enjoys travel and conductive materials seeking…" The feedback is tremendous. Then, as unexpectedly, I am myself again, straight as a plank and as boring as I put on my jeans without a spark, a zig or zag. Think: *Good Lord – the things it takes to just get by!*

About the Author

Robert Scotellaro is the author of 7 flash fiction collections including most recently: *Ways to Read the World* (Scantic Books, 2022) and *God in a Can* (Bamboo Dart Press, 2022), as well as 5 collections of poetry, and several books for children. He has, along with James Thomas, co-edited *New Micro: Exceptionally Short Fiction*, published by W.W. Norton & Co. His work has appeared widely, nationally and internationally, and is included in the W. W. Norton anthologies, *Flash Fiction International* (2015) and *Flash Fiction America* (2023), and in 4 *Best Small Fiction* and 2 *Best Microfiction* award anthologies. He is the winner of *Zone 3's* Rainmaker Prize in Poetry and the Blue Light Book Award for his fiction. Robert is one of the founding donors to The Ransom Flash Fiction Collection at the University of Texas, Austin. He currently lives in San Francisco with his wife, artist and art historian, Diana Scott. Find him at: www.robertscotellaro.com

www.ingramcontent.com/pod-product-compliance
Lightning Source LLC
Chambersburg PA
CBHW032152020726
47496CB00003B/846